The Welsh National Anthem

Key Eb

S.
A.

1. Mae   hen   wlad   fy
1. Oh!   land   of   my

Gwlad   beirdd   a   chan - tor - ion
The   home   of   the   Tel - yn;

The Welsh NATIONAL Anthem

Siôn T. Jobbins

y Lolfa

I Elliw, Gwenno ac Owain
– o bydded i'r ifanciaith barhau!

First impression: 2013

© Siôn T. Jobbins & Y Lolfa Cyf., 2013

Book and cover design: Y Lolfa
Cover photograph: Getty Images

ISBN: 978-1-84771-659-0

FSC

Published and printed in Wales
on paper from well managed forests
by Y Lolfa Cyf., Talybont, Ceredigion SY24 5HE
e-mail ylolfa@ylolfa.com
website www.ylolfa.com
tel 01970 832 304
fax 832 782

Hen Wlad fy Nhadau – Introduction

We are truly blessed to have 'Hen Wlad fy Nhadau' as our national anthem – it is an anthem of this land and for which we have fought to have it recognised.

It is a democratic anthem – it insults no one. It has no calls to conquer or humiliate others. It can be sung with gusto by people of all religions and none. It can have the allegiance of people of all political persuasions, be they communist, capitalist, monarchist or republican. It is not an embarrassing cringe-fest of adulation to a monarch or despot. It is humble without being coy.

Its tune is uplifting without being pompous or operatic. The tune can easily be sung by a child or can be given a full choral treatment.

Its final line 'o bydded yr heniaith barhau' – 'long may the old language [Welsh] endure' is so simple and humble

a wish, but it is a wish that the British state and their agents have been bent on denying. This simple refrain gives the anthem its bite. It reminds us that it is the Welsh language which makes us unique and allows us the right to call ourselves a nation. It reminds us that the language is more important than the state or the country or the head of state. It is the Welsh language which is our crown.

The anthem owes its success to the fact that it was never composed as an anthem.

In much the same way that a great statesman often has no wish to be a politician, a great anthem is often one composed with no higher ambition than to convey a deep felt feeling and to be sung. 'Hen Wlad fy Nhadau' spent a forty-year apprenticeship in the tough world of Welsh choral singing before it could dare to be considered a national anthem. It was not chosen by a committee or a government body or a monarch but by the jury of the Welsh nation, year after year, eisteddfod after eisteddfod, concert after concert. It was then, when the people had grown to love it and to appreciate the need for a national anthem to sing their existence as a nation to the world, that Hen Wlad fy Nhadau became our national anthem.

To find the history of 'Hen Wlad fy Nhadau' we have to go in search of a song called 'Glan Rhondda'.

< Sir Goscombe John's memorial statues at Ynys Angharad Park, Pontypridd. 10,000 people attended the unveiling in 1930
The preceding photograph of the memorial under snow was taken by Steve Tiley

The Local Song which became a National Song...

Like all great songs there is a romance about 'Hen Wlad fy Nhadau'. It is not an anthem born in the cold test tube of a competition but a genie which sprang from a bottle.

There is a myth about all good songs, and 'Hen Wlad fy Nhadau' is no exception. The first is what came first: the words or the tune? Was it Evan James, the shy, cultured father, who composed the lyrics along the banks of the Rhondda River on that Saturday afternoon on the 6th of January, 1856? Or was it his favourite son, James the harpist, who went for the stroll only to hurry back to his father's house in Mill Street and wake him, excited with his new tune? Did the father reach for his slate and chalk, which he always kept nearby for such moments of muse, and did he tell his son to fetch him a pint of beer from the nearby Colliers Arms, as was his wont when composing? Whatever the truth, the song was called 'Glan Rhondda' (the banks of the Rhondda), much as one would name a hymn tune. And 'Glan Rhondda' isn't a bad name for a song inspired by the river which, with the Taf, creates the elegant confluence on which Pontypridd is built.

On returning from chapel later that evening, James' mother Elizabeth chastised her son for playing music on the Sabbath. James stood his ground and reminded her that King David himself had also played the harp in the

Tabor Chapel, Maesteg, where the song was first sung

Sanctuary at the direct injunction of God himself.

The song was first performed publicly at the vestry of Tabor Chapel in Maesteg a month or so later by sixteen-year-old Elizabeth John of Pontypridd. It seems the song soon gained popularity. James James performed the song at a tavern eisteddfod in Ivor's Castle, Hopkinstown, and apparently children could be heard singing it on the streets of Pontypridd the following morning. It was certainly being sold in sheet form in the streets and fairs, as were other popular songs and ballads, because there is a copy at Pontypridd Library with '1858' pencilled on it. It would have been sung at a faster tempo than the one we are used to and James James made no effort to harmonise the new song.

That could have been the end of 'Glan Rhondda'. It could have joined the dozens of other songs that the Jameses composed and diligently wrote down in their little notebook, which is now kept at the National Library of Wales in Aberystwyth – songs that came and died with them.

If it had been lucky, 'Glan Rhondda' may have made it as a popular folk song, sung for a generation or two in eastern Glamorgan until the fashion of the age or the advance of the English language dislodged it from people's popular repertoire. That, for many a song, would be no mean feat. After all, there is no great dishonour in composing a song which is sung by others if only for a generation. Many composers would be very happy with such a modest success.

'Glan Rhondda' may then have been saved from extinction fifty years later by a bespectacled, diligent musicologist from the newly established Welsh Folk-Song Society.

But 'Glan Rhondda' weaved its way into the fabric of Welsh society.

The song was submitted for a competition for unpublished collections of Welsh airs at the famous 1858 Llangollen Eisteddfod by Thomas Llewelyn (Llewelyn Alaw – 'alaw' being Welsh for 'tune' or 'song'), a harpist from Llwyncoed, Aberdare and a friend of James James.

Llewelyn's collection won, earning him a princely £10 (more than £400 in today's money). Another anthology, submitted under the pseudonym of Orpheus, also included 'Glan Rhondda' and earned £5 consolation prize. Dr Meredydd Evans believes that Orpheus was none other than James James himself. The double exposure helped promote the song and was a nice little earner! The adjudicator, John Owen (or, to give his bardic name, Owain Alaw), asked for permission to include 'Glan Rhondda' in his publication *Gems of Welsh Melody* in 1860.

John Owen's *Gems of Welsh Melody*

This volume sold in great numbers and gave the song national recognition. Owain Alaw changed the title from the local 'Glan Rhondda', to the national 'Hen Wlad fy Nhadau' ('Old Land of my Fathers'). It was as if he understood the significance of the song where the James family had not. By changing from 'Rhondda' to 'Gwlad' he elevated the song from one of personal or local resonance to one that could touch the heart of any Welshman from any part of Wales.

Maybe one reason for its sudden chart-topping success was that as well as changing the title, Owain Alaw's published version was also adapted and weaved to suit the audience and new musical fashion.

As Dr Rhidian Griffiths notes, Owain Alaw adapted

the song for piano accompaniment and the chorus was arranged for four-part harmony. The tempo of the song was slowed down, too, from the folksong-like 6 / 8 time to a more sedate 3 / 4 time. This fitted the tastes of the newly energised eisteddfod culture as it moved from the tavern to the concert hall. The key was also changed from original F to E flat major. This was a master stroke – it is a popular key for Victorian hymn tunes and appeals to the dark, melancholic, almost Slavic mood of songs which are so popular with us Welsh.

Another significant change by Owain Alaw was the removal of the bar's rest which followed both declamations of 'Gwlad!' at the beginning of the chorus in the original version. This would have been the rest where a harpist, like James James, would have added their own improvised musical swirls.

These adaptations saw 'Glan Rhondda' change from being a folk song sung by individuals to 'Hen Wlad fy Nhadau' which could be sung by choirs and so fit into the mainstream of the Welsh chapel, choir and eisteddfod culture of Victorian Wales.

The song gained in popularity. In 1865 the *Aberystwyth Observer*, reporting on the National Eisteddfod of that year, referred to it as 'the national chorus, Hen Wlad fy Nhadau' but noted that the national anthem was sung separately. The following day, the eisteddfod was concluded with 'Hen Wlad fy Nhadau' sung in English and the next day

< Pontypridd as painted by Cedric Morris in 1945

'Rule Britannia' was the final song. It seems that national anthem in those days still meant 'God Save the Queen'.

From the 1870's onwards it became a regular feature to sing the anthem at the end of concerts or at an eisteddfod – as it still is. The song began to be seen increasingly as a national anthem, if not quite yet *the* national anthem.

...which became a National Anthem

'Hen Wlad fy Nhadau' had become popular but it faced a challenge from the awful 'God Bless the Prince of Wales', a song composed for the marriage of the English Prince of Wales (later Edward VII) to Alexandra of Denmark.

The Welsh words were written by the most famous and popular Welsh poet of the nineteenth century, John 'Ceiriog' Hughes, who was station clerk and manager of Van railway at Caersws, near Newtown. The music was composed by Henry Brinley Richards of Carmarthen, who won at the Gwent-Morgannwg eisteddfod of 1834 for his arrangement of the beautiful folk song, 'Llwyn Onn' ('Ash Grove') and who later studied under Chopin in Paris. It was first performed in 1863.

Like the James version of 'Hen Wlad fy Nhadau', it includes a romantic view of Wales so popular at the time. However, it fails for having no intimate connection with either the singer or with Wales.

Although 'God Bless the Price of Wales' was not composed in competition to 'Hen Wlad fy Nhadau', it did become for many, by proxy, a more British national song for Wales. It wished to appeal to the sentiment of royal family worship which disfigures Welsh life. But it is a song as turgid and limp as it is lacking in self-respect by any grown-up Welshman. It must say something about its grovelling tone that even the fawning Victorian Welsh never took to it with any great enthusiasm. It's interesting that the tune for 'God Bless the Prince of Wales' is also that of 'Derry's Walls', a Ulster Unionist song about the 1689 Siege of Derry sung by Glasgow Rangers football fans. This version actually benefits from being sung at a quicker folk tempo.

The song's lack of popularity may have something to do with Albert's dandy and adulterous reputation not being to Welsh Nonconformist taste. Is this why David Lloyd George used his political

Prince Albert, whom Lloyd George was keen to invest as Prince of Wales

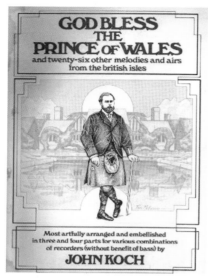

The opposition: the song *God Bless the Prince of Wales*

influence to invent the investiture of the new Prince of Wales in 1911? Was he aware of how lacking in support the title of Prince of Wales had become under Albert and thus saw the need to create a medieval pageant?

Albert, The Prince of Wales (who was confusingly then crowned Edward VII) as well as spawning a competing sycophantic song was also unwittingly instrumental in confirming 'Hen Wlad fy Nhadau' as Wales' national anthem.

In a rare act of defiance and self-respect, the Victorian Welsh managed to upstage the English Royal Family, thanks to 'Hen Wlad fy Nhadau'.

In 1887, the National Eisteddfod was held at the Royal Albert Hall in London. According to the historian John Davies, Queen Victoria famously spent seven years of her reign in Scotland, seven weeks in Ireland and seven days in Wales. Now that Wales had come to London, the Royal Family could hardly avoid it. Albert, as the so-called Prince of Wales, dutifully made an appearance.

He attended one of the eisteddfod's events on 12 August which commenced, as was the fashion, with 'God Bless the Prince of Wales'. Following the meeting, as the royal entourage began to leave, Eos Morlais ('the skylark of Morlais') led the singing of 'Hen Wlad fy Nhadau'. Either through embarrassment or duty, or confusion, the royals stopped and stood out of respect for the song. This 'Hallelujah chorus moment' as Rhidian Griffiths calls it, gave the Welsh the kind of royal approval they wished for. It was 'Hen Wlad fy Nhadau' 1 – Royal Family 0.

The Albert Hall incident coincided with the growth of Cymru Fydd (the Young Wales movement). It was the Welsh expression of nationalist movements such as Young Ireland that were rising across Europe, particularly in the Czech lands and other Slav and Baltic nations. Cymru Fydd worked within the Liberal Party networks and wished to see a Welsh parliament within the imperial family. It was inspired by such people as Mazzini of Italy and Kossuth of Hungary.

The campaign for a National Library and National Museum of Wales, the Welsh Folk-Song Society, and the University of Wales were part of this new patriotic Welsh confidence.

'Hen Wlad fy Nhadau' had come to express what it meant to be Welsh. The words were patriotic enough without being too political, and vague enough not to offend anyone. On 11 March 1899, it became one of the earliest Welsh songs to be recorded. Madge Breeze sang it

Hen Wlad fy Nhadau: an early recording by Decca

for the Gramophone Company in London, which pressed it to a single-sided seven-inch record lasting one minute and seventeen seconds. A scratchy, warbling Madge can still be heard on a CD copy produced by the National Screen and Sound Archive of Wales at the National Library.

In 1905, by the singing of the anthem, Wales made history. On 16 December 1905, 'Hen Wlad fy Nhadau' became the first national anthem to be sung at the start of a sporting event. But why this rugby match and not an earlier one? Is the date significant?

The game was played while Wales was still in the afterglow of the heady intoxicating 1904-05 Welsh Revival led by Evan Roberts. Roberts, a 26-year-old former collier from Loughor near Swansea, had become the main force of the Religious Revival that had swept across Wales, into the Welsh-speaking communities in Liverpool and as far as the Welsh colony in Patagonia. Coal miners held prayer meetings underground, some rugby clubs closed as people turned their backs on sport and drinking in favour of these exciting phenomena of music and religious experiences.

By 1905, and the international rugby match, the Revival had begun to fizzle out but one of its lasting legacies was the giving of a new breath of life to chapels and, by implication, hymn singing. Was this a contributing factor in the decision of the Welsh rugby players and crowd to answer the New Zealanders' haka dance with a rousing rendering of 'Hen Wlad fy Nhadau'?

Whatever the background, the Welsh wanted to beat the touring New Zealand team, which had been victorious in all its games so far. Wales had won the Triple Crown that year and the press eagerly, if bashfully, called this 'the Game of the Century'.

Hymn singing, and singing the anthem were popular during matches. On this famous day, however, Tom Williams, the Welsh Rugby Union's a d m i n i s t r a t o r, suggested that Wales player Teddy Morgan lead the crowd in the singing of 'Hen Wlad fy Nhadau' in response

Evan Roberts, leader of the 1904-05 religious revival

23

to the haka challenge. After Morgan began singing, the crowd joined in.

In addition to the intrinsic beauty of the song, it was a wise choice because he could be confident that the majority of the Welsh supporters would know the song and sing it well. Answering a war dance with four-part harmony – fantastic. In the same way that a well-executed haka dance shows self-respect, dedication and pride in one's culture, the Welsh anthem sung in four-part harmony should be a manly sign of our self-respect, dedication and pride in our culture.

In 1905 there were a million Welsh-speakers, and the majority of the crowd would probably have spoken Welsh. They would have known the song, they would have understood the words, and there was no need to have the words printed on a page or screen as today. Despite the last line of the anthem, 'o bydded i'r heniaith barhau', British rule has meant that the number of Welsh-speakers has decreased and a culture has weakened.

I cannot imagine a similar situation today where one could be confident that the crowd at a Welsh international would be able to sing any song, let alone one composed by one of their own nation, in unison and harmony. The crowd today can sing two lines of Max Boyce, 'and we were singing hymns and arias, Hen Wlad fy Nhadau, Ar Hyd y Nos' without actually singing any hymns or 'Ar Hyd y Nos' in their entirety. Our culture has become thinner, and we sing other people's songs about other people's countries – the kind of songs that are churned out during intervals at every rugby and football game today; the kind of songs that prevent us ever again having an '05 moment.

The singing of 'Hen Wlad fy Nhadau' before that historic rugby match, which Wales won, sealed the song for ever as the true anthem of Wales. Or did it?

It's not over till the Fat Man on the Terraces sings

Readers aged forty-five or older may remember the colonial habit of playing both 'Hen Wlad fy Nhadau' and 'God Save the Queen' at the beginning of Wales's rugby and football international matches.

Its sounds incredulous today but it happened well into the 1970s. It was if someone were saying, 'Okay, Taff, you can sing your little song but this is the proper grown-up anthem to remind you who's boss'.

In one respect, I do not blame the British establishment or the British mentality in Wales for thinking like this. After all, if Wales was not willing to fight for her independence what right does she have to make a fuss over singing the state anthem of Great Britain and Northern Ireland? If Wales does not like the anthem then she is free to leave the Union as the Irish have done.

With Wales it is a case of wanting it both ways; a rather unappealing side to our nationality. It is like the loser who is in the bully's gang because he is not brave enough to fight the bully. The loser projects his failings by siding with the bully in a kind of passive-aggressive relationship. I can respect the bullied man who fights back (like Ireland). I can even understand the bully, but there is nothing but ridicule and derision for this kind of Welshness; the

Welshness of the bully's sidekick, some yapping little dog.

In old footage of the rugby and football internationals, you will clearly hear the booing of 'God Save the Queen', although the commentators would try and play it down or possibly even turn the volume down.

Things came to a head in 1974 in what the historian Gareth Williams calls the 'year of the fuss'.

It had been decided for the 1973 rugby season not to play the 'God Save the Queen' as one of Wales's dual anthems at Cardiff and instead sing only 'Hen Wlad fy Nhadau'. The following year, 1974, when Wales played England at Twickenham, the (English) Rugby Football Union retaliated against the perceived snub by not playing 'Hen Wlad fy Nhadau' at all. However, while the band did not play the Welsh anthem, the Welsh crowd, like in 1905, sang the anthem as an act of defiance.

'God Save the Queen' continued to be played by the French authorities when Wales played there. France, which has never been sympathetic to smaller nations, especially if it could give hope to the Bretons, Basques or Catalans, would play the 'Queen' and the Welsh anthem. You can hear the crowd booing the English anthem in a clip of the 1977 game at Parc des Princes, which was captured as part of the raucous rugby classic TV film, *Grand Slam*.

The same 'fuss' happened at Wales' football matches. Change here happened gradually.

The Football Association of Wales decided not to play 'God Save the Queen' before the Wales match against

The film Grand Slam captured the booing of the English anthem

Austria on 19 November 1975. Why this game? Well, the rugby team had set a precedent and this game, like the 1905 New Zealand match, was billed as a very important game for Welsh football. The authorities wanted the full support of the crowd with no diversions.

But the British anthem was played in Welsh football games against Hungary and West Germany in 1976. In that game, the programme notes that 'God Save the Queen' would be played at the conclusion of the game while the players would stay on the field. This compromise arrangement was decided possibly because it had been expected that the Queen would be in attendance as patron of the Football Association of Wales in its centenary year.

But 'God Save the Queen' was on its wobbly last legs and into extra time. The Wales v Czechoslovakia game on 30 March 1977, in the Queen's Jubilee year, was the first international where it would not be played.

As with rugby, the change did not go totally unnoticed – not by the English FA at least. At Wembley in 1977, the England officials refused to play 'Hen Wlad fy Nhadau' during the Home International football match against Wales.

Phil Stead, author of *Welsh Dragons - the History of Welsh Football*, believes that this English act may have been in reaction to Wales' decision not to play 'God Save the Queen' during the match with Czechoslovakia. However, the Welsh players, led by John Mahoney and Terry Yorath, bravely remained in line in defiant protest after the rendition of 'God Save the Queen' despite the English officials' panic as they tried to usher the team away. As Phil noted, 'they only broke the line once they felt their point was made'.

It was a moment of pure drama, like the singing of 'La Marseillaise' in the classic wartime film *Casablanca*.

It was this kind of defiance, made even more poignant and beautiful by virtue of the fact that those brave football players could not speak Welsh, which gave the anthem the kind of war wounds every good anthem needs.

The defiance against authority, petty jobsworths and the OBE-eyeing establishment helped give 'Hen Wlad fy Nhadau' the cultural ballast that kept it sailing.

Footballers understand the importance of psychology. I would say that from 1977 onwards there has been no question that 'Hen Wlad fy Nhadau' is the national anthem of the Welsh. There is no other.

Wales and the World

Estonia and Finland do it; South Africa and New Zealand do it, and yes, even Great Britain and Lichtenstein do it.

What?

They share the same melody for their respective anthems.

And Wales does, too.

Our fellow Brythonic Celts, the Cornish and the Bretons, who speak a language similar to Welsh that also has mutations, sing their own version of 'Hen Wlad fy Nhadau'.

In Cornish, it's called 'Bro Goth agan Tasow', which is sung with Cornish words, composed by the father of the Cornish language revival, Henry Jenner (1848-1934). It competes with the popular and older 'Song of the Western Men' (also known as 'Trelawny's Song'), which is sung in English.

In Breton, the song is known as 'Bro Gozh ma Zadoù' and has a longer pedigree. It was initially brought to Breton shores by the Rev William Jenkyn Jones, a Welsh Protestant missionary sent to Brittany in 1882 to convert the Bretons from Catholicism to Protestantism. Jones translated the patriotic sentiments of the song into Breton but made the mistake of adding verses against the demon drink, which did not go down so well with the cider-pressing peasants of Penn-ar-Bed.

However, a young Breton patriot, Francois Jaffernou (or 'Taldir' to give his bardic name) revived the song. He was familiar with Wales and visited the National Eisteddfod at Cardiff in 1899 (where Patrick Pearse, one of the leaders of the Irish Easter Rising, was accepted to the Gorsedd). The recognised lyrics were published in 1898 in the patriotic Breton newspaper for which he wrote, *La Résistance*. It was chosen as a national anthem in 1903, the year of James James' death, at a conference of the Union Régionaliste Bretonne at Lesneven and was first recorded, by Pathé, in 1910.

During the 2009 French Cup final, which was played by two Breton teams, Stade Rennais and En Avant de Guingamp, the Bretons petitioned the French FA to have the anthem included in the proceedings. The French refused but allowed it to be sung before the official opening, giving the song greater exposure and status than it had ever received. Like Wales, sport was a way to unify and solidify the national identity.

But our fellow Celts are not the only ones who share our national anthem. Thanks (again) to Welsh missionaries, the Khasi people in Assam, north east India, have also adopted the same tune. The Welsh Christian mission began there in 1841 when Thomas Jones arrived in Cherrapunjee. He learnt the language and was the first to write it in Latin script. He then began translating the Bible into Khasi and sealed a long relationship and affinity between Wales and the Khasi. When the Mazo sub-tribe rebelled against Indian rule in the 1990s they did so on St David's Day.

I look forward to the day when we hear the tune of 'Hen Wlad fy Nhadau' played at international football and rugby matches between Wales and the other nations that share our anthem.

But is it a Proper National Anthem?

Saunders Lewis, never one to sit on the fence, was dismissive of 'Hen Wlad fy Nhadau'. The nationalist thinker and writer called it 'the most lying anthem in Europe'.

He was dismissive of those 80-minute patriots at the Arms Park or at a St David's Day dinner, who sang the anthem with a full

Saunders Lewis: dismissive

heart but who would also sing 'God Save the Queen' with equal, if not more, vigour.

Saunders Lewis was a Liverpool Welshman. He had re-learnt Welsh as a young man following his feeling of betrayal caused by fighting in the Great War. He saw that Ireland (and other small nations) had gained independence while the Welsh, who had been faithful to Britain, had gained nothing. He saw the dank hypocrisy of those politicians and public, Welsh speakers more than anyone, who sang 'o bydded i'r heniaith barhau' but did not speak Welsh to their children or who obstructed and campaigned against Welsh culture or status and education in Welsh.

But 'most lying anthem in Europe'? I am with Harri Webb on this. In a fluid and beautiful article on the anthem in 1964, the Merthyr librarian and poet believed old Saunders was being a little too harsh.

If the singer is insincere, that is not the fault of the anthem but a reflection of the singer. This ambivalance

Dafydd Iwan, composer of the stirring *Yma o Hyd*

has led some, from time to time, to suggest other anthems or seek other, stronger songs to compete with 'Hen Wlad fy Nhadau'.

Saunders (with Lewis Valentine) wrote Welsh words to *Finlandia,* that wonderful piece of music by the Finnish nationalist composer, Jean Sibelius.

Finlandia is certainly a magnificent and stirring melody and it encapsulates the fastness of the Finnish tundra and of Finnish history. It is often sung by choirs and its words, as one would expect by two devout Christians and nationalists, are unambiguous. But it has never challenged 'Hen Wlad fy Nhadau' nor, I guess, was it meant to. The words are too Christian for those who are not believers and 'Hen Wlad fy Nhadau' has already earned its place, whatever are Saunders' views of the song.

The melody of the Czech nationalist composer Bedřich Smetana, *Vlatava* in the second movement of his *Ma Vlast* (*My Country*), is one which is also often used in patriotic gatherings though, to my surprise, no Welshman has composed words to accompany this music.

There were other patriotic songs during the nineteenth century, some of which sound almost camp in their patriotism - certainly too melodramatic and romantic for modern ears. Songs like 'Mynyddoedd fy Ngwlad' ('The Mountains of My Country') are in a similar vein to 'Hen Wlad fy Nhadau'.

But 'Gŵyr Harlech' ('The Men of Harlech') would be the most likely challenger to 'Hen Wlad fy Nhadau' and is an older song. However, despite becoming a favourite with the military, being made famous in the 1964 film *Zulu* and being commonly sung in English, it has never come close to upstaging the James' anthem.

Maybe the words and the tune are too militaristic, maybe the talk of 'the Saxon's courage breaking' was a bit too strong for Welsh sensibilities, always afraid of offending the English. Ironically enough, its earliest printed version with words was included in Owain Alaw's 1860 *Gems of Welsh Melody* along with 'Hen Wlad fy Nhadau'.

In fact, there are many rousing patriotic songs in Welsh, with several composed during the national revival of 1960s onwards. 'Safwn yn y Bwlch' ('Into the Breach') by Glyn Roberts is popular with choirs, as is the spine-tingling

'O Gymru' by Rhys Jones and Aled Lloyd Davies. Dafydd Iwan's defiant 'Yma o Hyd' ('Still Here') has been adopted by rugby and football teams

Tich Gwilym; photo by Gerallt Llywelyn

across Wales and, as a sign of the change in Welsh society, is even played at Wales' international rugby matches and sung by Welsh football fans.

But 'Hen Wlad fy Nhadau' still reigns supreme. It is sung at the end of concerts and eisteddfodau and even at Welsh language rock gigs with defiant clenched fists held high. It was the title of Geraint Jarman a'r Cynghaneddwyr's rock album of 1978 in which the lead guitarist of the band, Rhondda-born Tich Gwilym, recorded an electric guitar rendition of the anthem in the spirit of Jimi Hendrix's version of the America's anthem, 'The Star Spangled Banner'.

The anthem is treated with the reverence it deserves at formal and social events. But it is also so well-liked that it is sung informally in pubs and at social gatherings – something Evan and James James would have liked, I am sure.

Evan and James James

The Welsh are not very good at recognising and celebrating their heroes.

We have a habit of believing that our heroes need to go before the great adjudication board in London before we can celebrate them at home. It seems that to be famous or to make a contribution within a Welsh context does not count.

But we are not always so lacking in self-esteem and respect.

A leisurely walk in Ynys Angharad Park in Pontypridd will bring you to two elegant statues. They are not statues of kings or queens or of soldiers who have killed Africans

The bronze relief of Evan and James James, which is part of Sir Goscombe John's memorial

in the name of empire. They are statues in celebration of a father and son, James James (1833 – 1902) and Evan James (1809 – 1878).

The graceful memorial was designed by Sir Goscombe John of Cardiff, who was one of Wales' foremost sculptors in the first half of the twentieth century.

His Pontypridd memorial includes a stylised Hellenic composer with a harp and a female singer and, between them, a bronze relief with the images of the father and son. It echoes another, earlier, elegant and peaceful war memorial by John which stands at Llandaf Cathedral Green in Cardiff.

Interestingly, the work may have inspired a memorial to two other influential Welsh father and son – Owen M. Edwards and Ifan ab Owen Edwards in Llanuwchllyn, near Bala. Owen Edwards, an MP, did much to fight for Welsh language and social rights and his son, Ifan, formed the Welsh language youth movement, the Urdd, in 1922.

So who were these Pontypridd composers whose statues grace the town, Evan and James James?

In keeping with the tradition of the age, they also had bardic names; Ieuan ab Iago and Iago ab Ieuan. These were names they would have used for eisteddfodic competitions and concerts. The bardic names were part of the Romantic movement of the nineteenth century that swept across Europe and gave new life to other small nations like the Czechs, Slovenes and Estonians. In Wales, it inspired such people as Iolo Morganwg from the Vale of Glamorgan.

Iolo Morganwg: Welsh romantic from the Vale of Glamorgan

Evan James's bardic name was Ieuan ab Iago. His son was Iago ab Ieuan. The 'ab' means 'son of', like the Scottish 'mac'. It's more commonly spelt as 'ap' but it's an 'ab' if the name following it starts with a vowel.

The 'ap' or 'ab' was the favoured way of naming sons in Wales until the late middle ages. That's because under Welsh Law, a person had to know their genealogy, as the whole extended family could be held responsible for their crimes. An extended family included anyone related to you back to the eighth generation. With the imposition of English Law in 1536 and 1542, Welsh law, the Laws of Hywel Dda, was replaced. However, by the nineteenth century, the use of the 'ap' offered the person an air of medieval princely status and a link with an unbroken and proud poetic tradition. It was also, no doubt, in a Wales full to the brim of Jones, Williams, Davies and James, a useful way of identifying people!

But Ieuan ab Iago and Iago ab Ieuan were far from being princes.

They were the embodiment of what in Welsh is called the 'gwerin'. 'Gwerin' is often translated in English as 'working class' but that doesn't convey the true meaning. The German 'volk' or Slavic 'narod' are closer to the Welsh meaning. That is, in nineteenth century Wales, the term would have referred to that great mass of the population of Wales which was Welsh-speaking, working for a living (as opposed to the gentry) and probably Nonconformist rather than Anglican. In 1856, the 'gwerin' meant most

A romantic view of Pontypridd bridge as painted by Turner in 1798

people in Wales. It is for this reason that the Welsh word for republic is 'gweriniaeth' – government of the mass of the people not of the gentry.

The 'gwerin', as well as being the workers, liked to think of themselves as being cultured too. The James family were certainly a part of this working class tradition.

Evan James, the father, was born in Caerffili. He married Elizabeth Stradling, who was from the famous and cultured Glamorgan minor gentry family. Evan set up a weaving shed at the Ancient Druid Inn in Bedwellty on the Glamorgan-Gwent border. With his son, James (could he not have chosen another name?), he moved to the booming town of Pontypridd to set up his business at the 'factory' on Mill Street. The building is now, sadly, demolished, but the plaque has been placed at the nearby council offices.

Welsh would have been the predominant language of the town. The Rhondda Valley in 1856 would have been like the Ystwyth or Rheidol Valley today – pastoral and tranquil. Pontypridd was a chopsy market town, fast becoming an industrial hub. It was also full of Welsh intellectuals and interesting people with a lively, bickering cultural scene based on eisteddfodau and poetic and musical recitals in pubs – what was called by some contemporaries as 'Clic y Bont' or 'The Pontypridd Clique'.

In many ways, the year 1856 sat between two epochs.

The Merthyr Riots of 1831, after which Dic Penderyn had been unjustly hanged at Cardiff gaol (where Cardiff

Market now stands), the Chartist March on Newport of 1839 and the Rebecca Riots of the 'hungry 1840s' were all contemporaneous of Evan James. One famous contemporary was Dr William Price, the mad genius physician of nearby Llantrisant, who was a vegetarian, druid and nationalist and named and cremated his son Iesu Grist (Jesus Christ). He baptised his daughter at the Maen Chwyf (Rocking Stone) in Pontypridd and, in 1855, led a parade of Ivorites through the streets of

Dr Richard Price, trailblazing radical

Merthyr Tudful, accompanied by a half-naked man calling himself Myrddin (Merlin) and a goat.

The Iforiaid ('The Philanthropic Order of True Ivorites'), was a mutual society formed in Wrexham in 1836 and were very active in the south. Evan was a member. It was the only friendly society that conducted its business exclusively in Welsh and also, deliciously, had its own secret code of handshakes. Its laws and regulations state that it was there 'to encourage the Welsh language, to preserve its member as far as possible from want'. It was named after Ifor Hael (Ifor the Generous), the fourteenth century nobleman who resided at Bassaleg, near Newport, who was a great patron of the arts and was a sponsor of Wales' greatest medieval poet, Dafydd ap Gwilym.

Against this quasi-republican, radical background stood the eccentric and fantastic legacy of Iolo Morganwg and druidism. Pontypridd seems to have been a hotbed of druids and, frankly, eccentric people. Myfyr Morganwg (Evan Davies) was a self-educated man of Pencoed, near Bridgend, who set up as a watchmaker in Pontypridd. He believed Christianity was Druidism in Jewish clothing and held ceremonies on the two equinoxes and two solstices at the Maen Chwyf at Pontypridd. By coincidence, his son would marry Elizabeth John, the young girl who first performed 'Hen Wlad fy Nhadau' publicly at Tabor Chapel.

On the one side of 1856 was the world of Pontypridd inhabited by the mad quasi-republicans, proto-nationalists and Dewi Alaw's estimation of 139 poets with their word play and suspicion of authority. On the other side was the oncoming, suffocating tsunami of 'parchusrwydd' (respectfulness) with its humiliation of Welsh, monarchical worship and puritanism of High Victorian Wales.

The Dafydd Morgan Religious Revival would happen in 1859, which leads one to ask whether James James would have dared rebuke his God-fearing mother had he composed the tune on a Sunday three years later?

The Government Report into Education in Wales, which, in Welsh, is called 'Brad y Llyfrau Gleision' ('the Treachery of the Blue Books') was written in 1847, but was not translated into Welsh until 1852 in the *Traethodydd* magazine. The report was written to find out the nature of education in Wales but its findings and remarks against the morals of the Welsh, and especially the morals of the Welsh language, cast a long shadow over Welsh life.

The report is a fascinating document but the attitude of its commissioners and many of the English establishment in Wales whom they interviewed was classically colonial. Among its many comments concerning the Welsh language was, 'The Welsh language is a vast drawback to Wales and a manifold barrier to the moral progress and commercial prosperity of the people'. The psychological effects of the report were such that the esteemed Labour historian, Prof Kenneth O. Morgan, referred to the significance of the report and its consequence as 'the Glencoe and the Amritsar of Welsh history'.

While other nations would have stuck up two fingers at the report, the Welsh internalised it. They agreed with the psychology of the colonisers, and saw Welsh as a hindrance and felt that Wales should adopt the English language in the name of progress and civilisation.

Michael D. Jones of Bala became so depressed by the deliberate British policy to make Wales an English language province that he sought to build a new Wales in Patagonia. In 1865, the *Mimosa* ship would sail out of Liverpool with 150 people aboard, determined to establish a Welsh colony where Welsh would be the language of education, the law, religion and social life – the things it could not be in Wales, thanks to British rule.

ANTHEM OF WALES.

THE NATION'S DEBT OF HONOUR.

LONG DELAYED MEMORIAL.

AN APPEAL THAT DESERVES A PROMPT RESPONSE.

Much to the discredit of all Welshmen who claim to be sincere nationalists, the fund for the erection of a memorial to the authors of " Hen Wlad fy Nhadau " is still £400 short of the required sum.

There has been no lack of effort on the part of the promoters, but the outbreak of war in 1914 and post-war conditions have deprived the fund of the necessary response, and the committee are somewhat disheartened.

EVAN JAMES (Ieuan ap Iago), author of the words.

JAMES JAMES, his son, composer of the music.

Another attempt is now being made to bring the scheme to fruition, and an earnest appeal is made to readers of the *Western Mail & South Wales News* throughout the Principality, and further afield, to subscribe the sum of £400, which will bring the fund up to £2,250, the cost of the memorial which Sir W. Goscombe John, R.A., has been commissioned to erect in Ynysangharad Park, Pontypridd.

There ought to be no difficulty in securing this · comparatively small amount among so large a circle. Everyone sympathises with the movement; the trouble is that sympathy is not enough, and that people do not apply the appeal to themselves personally. Our readers are urged to respond quickly, and according to their means.

The story of Evan and James James, the father and son who endowed the nation with its pæan of racial pride, is given below, and the Welsh man or woman who reads it without sending a subscription, large or small, to the fund must not cavil if critics of the Welsh nation become caustic.

46

Writing the words of the anthem in 1856, four years after most Welsh speakers would have been aware of the report, was Evan James' defence of his language a coincidence? Was he in some way reacting to the Blue Books and a growing anti-Welsh language sentiment?

Was it decisive that Pontypridd was also in the border area between English and Welsh, a town where the Welsh-speakers must have been more sensitive to what could be lost? After all, two years after 'Hen Wlad fy Nhadau' was composed, the Ivorites changed their rules, stating that their secretaries should be competent in record keeping in both Welsh and English. Evans James would have been aware of how Cardiff, only twelve miles south, was changing linguistically. Welsh was the language of just over half the Sunday schools, but the tide was turning. Evan would have had personal experience of how the Welsh language was weakening, especially as more English (and Irish) immigrants moved in.

Is that one reason why the anguish expressed in the words can still be felt today? Are we not still, as a nation, on the border or precipice of losing our unique culture and language? The words to 'Hen Wlad fy Nhadau', then, are a particular reaction by a particular man from a particular part of Wales.

When one considers the fantastical and mad ideas floating about Pontypridd at the time, and the creeping

< A press cutting telling the story of the efforts to raise money for the memorial

anglophilia, Evan James' words are surprisingly clear-headed, down-to-earth and sensible. That is one reason why they have withstood the test of time and changing faces of fashion and politics.

The Words

Mae hen wlad fy nhadau yn annwyl i mi
Gwlad beirdd a chantorion, enwogion o fri
Ei gwrol ryfelwyr, gwladgarwr tra mad
Tros ryddid collasant eu gwaed
Gwlad, gwlad, pleidiol wyf i'm gwlad
Tra môr yn fur i'r bur hoff bau
O bydded i'r heniaith barhau.

The tune may have been adapted but the words to 'Hen Wlad fy Nhadau' are the one aspect of the song which has stayed constant in its 150-year history.

There are three verses but it is only the first that is usually sung. The two other verses are a little too romantic for modern tastes and, in any case, singing one verse of any national anthem at a public function in any language is more than enough.

It is believed Evan James, a pacifist and a follower of the English radical, Tom Paine, composed the words in answer to his brother, who had emigrated to America and was tempting Evan to join him in the New World. If so, one can read the words as one person's manifesto explaining why he should stay true to his fatherland.

And there we are, straight into the first incongruous thing about the anthem. In Welsh we say 'mamwlad' (motherland) but the anthem is 'Gwlad fy nhadau' (land of my fathers; 'tadau' has been mutated to 'nhadau'). There is no such word as 'tadwlad' in Welsh.

So, why did Evan James use this phrase? You would say 'cyn-deidiau' (literally, fore-grandfathers) for the word 'ancestors' in Welsh and he may have alluded to that. Maybe, too, in a slightly misogynistic way, Evan James thought 'Hen wlad fy mamau' just didn't sound right.

Staying with the first line, isn't the word 'annwyl' (dear) interesting?

It is such a tender word to use for an anthem, though, of course, the words were never composed with the intention of being a national anthem. 'Annwyl' is a tactile, dare I say feminine word, which instantly makes the anthem more personal and less boastful than most written-to-order national anthems.

If the story of Evans James trying to answer his brother's call to emigrate to America is true, then, it is not too fanciful to imagine that the word 'annwyl' would have been on his mind. After all, his letter would have started with 'Annwyl...'

Evan then proceeds to say why the land is 'annwyl' to him. The other verses describe the geography of the land, but the first verse says 'gwlad beirdd a chantorion, enwogion o fri' – 'land of poets and singers, famous and renowned'.

Being a 'poet and singer', you would expect Evan to place these before soldiers and monarchs. And, after all, if he did emigrate to America, what would he do? Of course, he could continue to be a weaver but as any writer will tell you, that is just the day job to pay the bills. Who would want to hear Welsh poetry or Welsh harp music in the New World?

But is this not also part of the beauty of the anthem? Evan James elevates culture above states; music above conquest; poetry above kings and queens. He goes further, I believe. He equates those who promote Welsh language culture as soldiers for their country.

'Ei gwrol ryfelwyr, gwladgarwyr tra mad' – can be sung as a new and different line, but can also be read as an extension of the preceding line. Imagine a hyphen after 'fri'. It would read as 'land of poets and singers, famous and renowned – her manly warriors; patriots so fine'.

That is, those who compose in Welsh are warriors for the language, as brave and as important as any soldier. I would concur with this sentiment. We are all soldiers, in our own way, for the Welsh language when we speak it and use it.

Is there also another image lying in Evan's subconscious?

One of the iconic Welsh images of the time was the heroic image of the last bard by Thomas Jones, which is at the National Museum in Cardiff. In the painting of 1774, the bard is poised on the edge of the cliff clutching a harp. He is the last surviving Welsh bard and he places a curse upon the English before leaping to his death. The dramatic painting is based on Thomas Gray's poem, 'The

The Last Bard, painting by Thomas Jones in 1774

Bard' and it tells the tale of Edward I's legendary massacre of the Welsh bards as he conquered Wales in 1282.

A similar heroic but more defiant image of the bard appears as an etching on the cover of Edward Jones' (Bardd y Brenin) famous publication of 1784, *Musical and Poetical Relations of the Welsh Bards*. Again, it is based on Thomas Gray's poem 'The Bard'.

As a harpist and a cultured person, Evan James must have been aware of this image, especially that of Edward Jones' book, which included so many Welsh songs. Did he imagine himself in the lineage of the 'last bard' defending Wales and her culture?

We then come to the line which proves beyond doubt, not that there is any, that Evans James was a Valleys Man. The giveaway sign is the word 'gwaed' (blood).

This is usually sung in the accepted standard Welsh form, with both the 'a' and 'e' in 'gwaed' pronounced equally. But Evans Jones was a Hwntw (south Walian) and he would have pronounced 'gwaed' as 'gwâd'. More probably still, he would have said it in the Welsh accent of Glamorgan and Gwent as an 'a denau' ('thin a'). That is, the 'a' was pronounced more as an 'e'. So 'mad' would be 'med' and 'gwaed' would be 'gwed'. It's this accent which some believe is the basis for the hard 'a' in the Cardiff English accent. But 'thin a' or 'open a' it then rhymes nicely with the last word in the preceding line, 'mad' (pronounced with a long 'a' too).

Although he wrote in standard Welsh, Evan would never have said 'gwaed'. He possibly would not have been aware of a pronunciation or would have forgotten that others in the north pronounced it differently. In any case, this was initially a personal song for a local audience.

So, when singing this line it would be more correct to sing 'gwâd' not 'gwaed'.

We then come to the famous chorus. As Harri Webb noticed, it is interesting that in the whole three verses 'Cymru' is only said once, whereas 'gwlad' is sung fifteen times. You would maybe expect 'Cymru' to be in the

54

chorus… but that comprises two syllables where Evan only has space for one. He then makes a brave and bold statement – almost a challenge to the listener; 'pleidiol wyf i'm gwlad'.

'Pleidiol' comes from 'plaid'. Plaid, of course, is the modern Welsh word for a political party as in Plaid Cymru or Plaid Lafur. It means choosing side, being partisan. It is difficult to translate, but what Evan is saying is that he is 'partisan to his country'. Old dictionaries also describe 'plaid' as meaning 'pledge'. That is why it is such a strong statement to imprint on the side of the pound coin.

Evan is drawing his line in the sand. He is telling his brother that he is staying put in Wales. The words are a pledge to this land, "Look, this is an oath. Don't sing these words if you don't take that pledge seriously. You can't sing this song and pledge publicly that you are a partisan and then swan off and sing 'God Save the Queen' ".

But then, Evan introduces some uncertainty into the words. This has become the topic of some discussion over the years in nationalist circles as we sing 'tra môr yn fur i'r bur hoff bau' ('whilst the sea is a wall for the pure loved land').

That is, the sea is our defence. Fine but, well, Wales is surrounded on only three sides by the sea – it is not an island. So, is Evan referring here to Britain the island as the 'pure country' or is he, as Harri Webb believed, saying that

< The Welsh spirit marvellously depicted by Evan Walters in a poster for the National Eisteddfod of 1926 in Swansea

the sea is the defence on three sides and then the language, which is alluded to in the next line, the fortification for the other, eastern, side?

Maybe Evan just liked the alliteration and did not think much of it. Maybe, as was the case, he saw Wales as his country but Britain as the state which defended her from foreign invasion (read Catholics, those damned Frenchies and Bonaparte). Maybe Evan is saying, 'Yes, we'll stick with being a part of Britain but we want to be respected as Welsh speakers'. In an age when a political and constitutional concept of Wales was very weak, people like Evan would shift their idea of 'country' – meaning Wales or meaning Britain. If this was the case, then Evan was wrong to put his faith in Britain as, under British rule, his language, Welsh, has not been defended and has declined from an estimated 80% of the population in Evan's time to 20% today. The British state will defend many things but the Welsh language is not one of them.

This line is doubly delicate and delicious as it is almost also pure Latin; 'tra môr yn fur i'r bur hoff bau' – 'dum mare marus pagus ita pura' in my cod Latin translation.

Yes, a bored Roman centurion in drizzly Isca, or Caerleon, would understand the gist of this line. That is because when the Romans came here two thousand years ago, ancient Welsh was the native language of the whole of Wales and England, and we Welsh adopted a lot of Latin words into our everyday speech.

The words *môr* (sea), *mur* (wall), *pur* (pure) and *pau*

(land, which has been mutated to *bau*) are Latin.

The word 'pau' is the same word as the French 'pays' as in their name for us, Pays de Galles, and is pronounced the same. It comes from 'pagus' and is ultimately the same word as 'pais' in Spanish, which also gives us the name for the county of Powys. They are all variations on marked land or administered territory.

'Pau' is not a word much used today, and when it is, it is usually used to signify a domain. But it was used because it rhymes with 'parhau' ('continue'). And this is where, for me and thousands of others, we come to the most important line in the anthem; 'o bydded i'r heniaith barhau' – 'long may the old language endure'.

This is a fantastic line… but this also leaves me a little unsettled, if not underwhelmed. 'Parhau'? 'Endure'? What, is that it? Things which are pickled endure. Why not sing that we want Welsh to 'thrive' or 'prosper' or 'grow' … rather than just endure?

This lets a lot of politicians and weak-willed Welsh people off the hook. How many of those who blast out this line at the Millennium Stadium are happy for Welsh to 'endure' but won't do anything active to promote it or stand up for it? As long as the language endures – a bit of Welsh here and there – then 'it's, okay, eh, boys?' Is that the sum of our ambition as a nation? Is that not a bit defensive and weak? Would the English have allowed their language to be spoken by only 20% of their population? I think not.

But still 'o bydded i'r heniaith barhau' is the most

important line in the anthem. I will give old Evan the benefit of the doubt – he wanted a future for the Welsh language, but he also needed a rhyme. It's a fantastic crescendo.

This line and this sentiment has sustained and challenged people for over 150 years. The tune is noble and popular and I wish this anthem would be played when next a Welsh athlete stands on an Olympic podium. It is an anthem worthy of our nation – are we worthy of it?

We should sing the words loud, in harmony and often, for it is of this land which is ours.

Not bad for a weaver and his son from Pontypridd.

The music

Mae Hen Wlad fy Nhadau
Welsh National Anthem

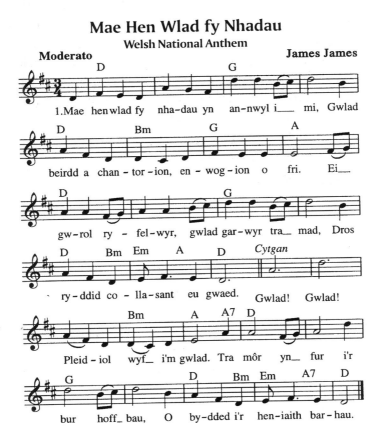

The Welsh words

Mae hen wlad fy nhadau yn annwyl i mi,
Gwlad beirdd a chantorion, enwogion o fri;
Ei gwrol ryfelwyr, gwladgarwyr tra mad,
Dros ryddid collasant eu gwaed.

(Cytgan – *Chorus*)

> Gwlad, gwlad, pleidiol wyf i'm gwlad.
> Tra môr yn fur i'r bur hoff bau,
> O bydded i'r hen iaith barhau.

Hen Gymru fynyddig, paradwys y bardd,
Pob dyffryn, pob clogwyn, i'm golwg sydd hardd;
Trwy deimlad gwladgarol, mor swynol yw si
Ei nentydd, afonydd, i mi.

(Cytgan – *Chorus*)

Os treisiodd y gelyn fy ngwlad tan ei droed,
Mae hen iaith y Cymry mor fyw ag erioed,
Ni luddiwyd yr awen gan erchyll law brad,
Na thelyn berseiniol fy ngwlad.

(Cytgan – *Chorus*)

English translation

This land of my fathers is dear to me
Land of poets and singers, and people of stature
Her brave warriors, fine patriots
Shed their blood for freedom

(Cytgan – *Chorus*)

> Land! Land! I am true to my land!
> As long as the sea serves as a wall for this pure,
> dear land
> May the language endure for ever.

Old land of the mountains, paradise of the poets,
Every valley, every cliff a beauty guards;
Through love of my country, enchanting voices will be
Her streams and rivers to me.

(Cytgan – *Chorus*)

Though the enemy have trampled my country underfoot,
The old language of the Welsh knows no retreat,
The spirit is not hindered by the treacherous hand
Nor silenced the sweet harp of my land.

(Cytgan – *Chorus*)

Phonetic version

My hair-n wool-add ver n-had eye
Un ann-will ee me
Gool-ard buy-rth ah chant-or-yon
En-wog-yon oh vree
Eye goo-rol ruv-elle-weir
Gool-ard garr-weir trah-mahd
Tross ruh-thid coll-ass-ant eye gwide

(Cytgan – *Chorus*)

     Gool-ard, gool-ard
     Ply-dee-ol oiv eem gool-ard
     Trah more un veer eer bee-rr hore-ff buy
     Oh buthed eer hen-yithe barr-high

Selected Bibliography

Harri Webb – *A Militant Muse, Selected Literary Journalism 1948-80* Edited by Meic Stephens (Seren Press, 1998)

Gwyn Griffiths – *Gwlad fy Nhadau: Ieuan, Iago, eu Hoes a'u Hamser* (Carreg Gwalch, 2006)

Rhidian Grifith – *Hen Wlad fy Nhadau in its Musical Context,* lecture published in Morgannwg, The Journal of Glamorgan History, vol.51 (2007)

Huw Walters – *Cynnwrf Canrif: Agweddau ar Ddiwylliant Gwerin* (Cyhoeddiadau Barddas, 2004)

The Welsh National Anthem is just one of a wide range of books of Welsh interest published by Y Lolfa. For a full list of books currently in print, simply surf into our website where you can browse and order on-line, and even order a paper catalogue.

www.ylolfa.com

TALYBONT CEREDIGION CYMRU SY24 5AP
e-mail ylolfa@ylolfa.com
phone (01970) 832 304
fax 832 782